Fiddle Time Runners

Piano accompaniment book

Kathy and David Blackwell

Teacher's note
These piano parts are written to accompany the tunes in *Fiddle Time Runners*. They are an alternative to the violin duet accompaniments or audio tracks, and are not designed to be used with those items. These parts may be used with violins playing together with violas (using *Viola Time Runners* and playing the ensemble parts where appropriate); a separate viola piano accompaniment book is available providing parts for all the additional tunes in *Viola Time Runners*.

Kathy and David Blackwell

OXFORD
UNIVERSITY PRESS

OXFORD
UNIVERSITY PRESS

Great Clarendon Street, Oxford OX2 6DP,
United Kingdom

Oxford University Press is a department of the University of Oxford.
It furthers the University's objective of excellence in research, scholarship,
and education by publishing worldwide. Oxford is a registered trade mark of
Oxford University Press in the UK and in certain other countries

Impression: 1

ISBN: 978-0-19-356615-6

Cover illustration by Martin Remphry

Music and text origination by Katie Johnston and Julia Bovee
Printed in Great Britain

Contents

1. Start the show

KB & DB

13
f
f
17
mf cresc.
mf cresc.
f
f
21
mf
mf
25
f
f

2. Banyan tree

Jamaican folk tune

3. Heat haze

KB & DB

Relaxed

4. Medieval tale

KB & DB

5. Cornish May song

Cornish folk tune

Lively

6. Chase in the dark

KB & DB

7. Merrily danced the Quaker's wife

Scottish folk tune

8. O leave your sheep: page 14

9. Jazzy Jingle bells

J. Pierpont

Nos. 8 and 9 are reversed to avoid a page turn.

21
1.
2.
Fine
cresc.
f
cresc.
f
25
mf
mf
30
35
D.𝄋 al Fine
cresc.
cresc.

8. O leave your sheep

French folk tune

10. Allegretto in G

Mozart

11. The Mallow fling

Irish folk tune

12. Noël

Daquin

13. Finale from the 'Water Music'

Handel

14. Ecossaise in G

Beethoven

15. Fiddle Time rag

KB & DB

Not too fast

17
f
f
mp
mp
22
27
mf
mf
32
cresc.
cresc.
f
f
8vb

16. Busy day

KB & DB

17. On the go!

KB & DB

* The repeat is written out in full in the violin part.

18. Yodelling song: page 26

19. Takin' it easy

KB & DB

* The repeat is written out in full in the violin part.
Nos. 18 and 19 are reversed to avoid a page turn.

17
21
mf
25
poco rit.
cresc.
cresc.
CODA
41
pizz.
p
p

18. Yodelling song

German folk tune

With a strong beat

20. Romani band

KB & DB

Fiery!

21. Ten thousand miles away

With a good swing

Sea shanty

13
Fine
cresc.
cresc.
(16)
mp
mp
mf
mf
21
f
f
25
D.C. al Fine

22. I got those fiddle blues

KB & DB

13
16
20
24
rall.

23. Air in G

J. C. Bach

24. Prelude from 'Te Deum'

Charpentier

25. That's how it goes!

KB & DB

13
16
mp
mp
19
cresc.
cresc.
22
D.C. al Fine
f
f

26. Hari coo coo

27. Summer evening

KB & DB

28. Flamenco dance

KB & DB

mp
mp
pizz.
f
f
arco
f
f
cresc.
ff
marcato cresc.
ff

29. Adam in the garden

Jamaican folk tune

Relaxed tempo

21
f
f
27
f
f
33
mp
mp
39
f
f

30. Somebody's knocking at your door

Spiritual

31. The old chariot

Sea shanty

32. Air

Handel

33. The wee cooper o' Fife: next page

34. Winter song

KB & DB

Wistfully

Nos. 33 and 34 are reversed to avoid a page turn.

33. The wee cooper o' Fife

Scottish folk tune

13
mf
mp
16
20
cresc.
cresc.
mf
24
Slower
4
4
mp
p

35. Rory O'More

Lively

Traditional Irish Jig

36. Trick cyclist: next page

37. Aerobics!

KB & DB

Nos. 36 and 37 are reversed to avoid a page turn.

36. Trick cyclist

KB & DB

With energy

15
pizz.
p
arco
mp
p stacc.
mp
18
cresc.
f
cresc.
f
21
mp
cresc.
mp
cresc.
24
LH pizz.
mf cresc.
f
p
mf cresc.
f
p

38. Caribbean sunshine

KB & DB

Calypso